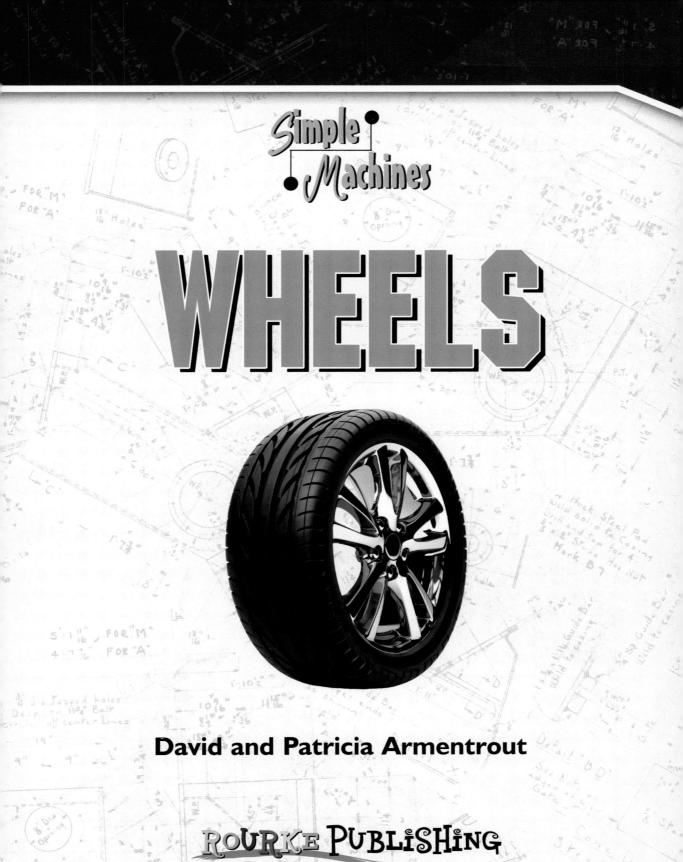

Simple Machines

WHEELS

David and Patricia Armentrout

ROURKE PUBLISHING

Vero Beach, Florida 32964

www.rourkepublishing.com

PHOTO CREDITS: © BlackJack3D: Title Page; © morganl: 5; © Trevor Hunt: 5, 9, 21; © Christian Lupu: 6; © Julia Nichols: 7; © David Morgan: 7; © filonmar: 7, 20; © Dave Long: 8; © Rich Legg: 9; © Thomas Perkins: 10; © DNY59: 11; © digitalskillet: 12; © Lisa Turay: 13; © Armentrout: 14, 15; © Michael Newell: 16 (flame); © Brian McEntire: 17; © Tarek El Sombati: 18; © Raoul Vernede: 19; © ernestking: 20; © Denis Radovanovic: 21; © Long Ha: 22

Edited by Kelli Hicks

Cover designed by Renee Brady

Interior designed by Tara Raymo

Library of Congress Cataloging-in-Publication Data

Armentrout, David, 1962-
  Wheels / David and Patricia Armentrout.
    p. cm. -- (Simple machines)
  Previous ed. by Patricia Armentrout under title: Wheel.
  ISBN 978-1-60694-392-2 (hard cover)
  ISBN 978-1-60694-524-7 (soft cover)
  1. Wheels--Juvenile literature. I. Armentrout, Patricia, 1960- II.
Armentrout, Patricia, 1960- Wheel. III. Title.
  TJ181.5.A76 2009
  621.8--dc22
                          2009006071

ROURKE PUBLISHING

www.rourkepublishing.com - rourke@rourkepublishing.com
Post Office Box 643328 Vero Beach, Florida 32964

TABLE OF CONTENTS

MACHINES

Machines are great because they help people do work with less effort. The **wheel** and **axle,** lever, pulley, inclined plane, wedge, and screw are machines. They are simple machines. Simple machines have few or no moving parts. Smart people have learned to combine simple machines to make **complex machines.**

Complex machines like elevators, school buses, and toasters have many moving parts.

WHEEL AND AXLE

Wheels are familiar to all of us. Look around; they are everywhere. Bicycles, cars, and even vacuum cleaners have wheels. Everyone uses them, but what do you really know about wheels? For starters, they are round. Wheels also come in many sizes: big wheels, small wheels, fat wheels, and skinny wheels.

small

skinny

big

To be a true simple machine, a wheel needs an axle. An axle is a shaft or rod in the center of a wheel. The wheel turns on the axle. An axle can also connect two wheels so they can work together. How can wheels and axles make our work easier?

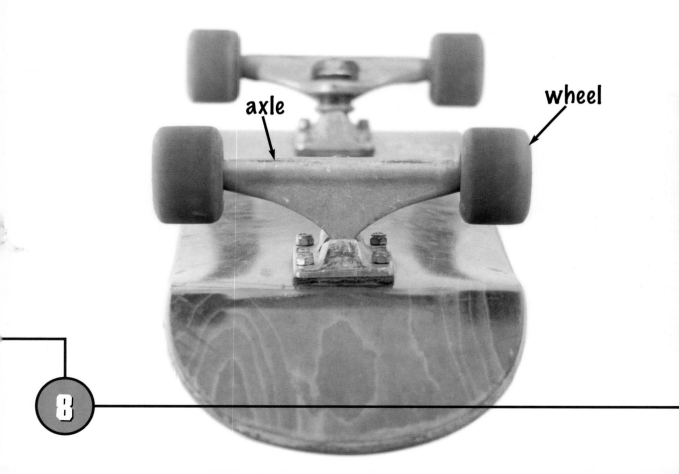

axle

wheel

gear

Gears are wheels with teeth that link with other gears,
or other devices such as bicycle chains.

MECHANICAL ADVANTAGE

Wheels and axles, as with all simple machines, have one thing in common. They make our work easier by giving us a **mechanical advantage.** A person using a simple machine can do the same amount of work with less effort. Most everyone would agree that's a big advantage.

A hand truck makes the task of moving several boxes quicker and easier.

For example, let's say it's your job to harvest pumpkins from the garden. Can you drag them across the ground? Maybe, but they are heavy. What could you use to make your work easier? Try loading the pumpkins into a wheelbarrow. It is easier to use a wheelbarrow than it is to drag the pumpkins. A wheelbarrow has a wheel and axle to share the weight, also called the load. The wheel and axle gives you a mechanical advantage.

Wheelbarrows make work easier on flat surfaces buy trying to push a wheelbarrow up a hill makes work harder.

WHEELS AND FRICTION

When two objects rub against each other, they create **friction.** Friction slows movement.

Imagine dragging a garbage can down the driveway. The can scrapes noisily along as you pull. The noise comes from friction between the bottom of the can and the driveway.

The more friction there is, the harder it is to pull the can. Would wheels make the job easier? You bet. It is easier to roll a heavy object than it is to drag it along. Wheels reduce friction.

More Friction

Less Friction

Do you Understand Friction?

Pretend you are competing in a soapbox derby race. You can choose between two cars. One is shiny and red with painted yellow flames and square wheels. The other is gray and dented, and has four big, round wheels. Which car do you choose?

You want to win, so of course you choose the car with round wheels. The red car looks cool, but you know square wheels would create too much friction. Besides, who ever heard of square wheels?

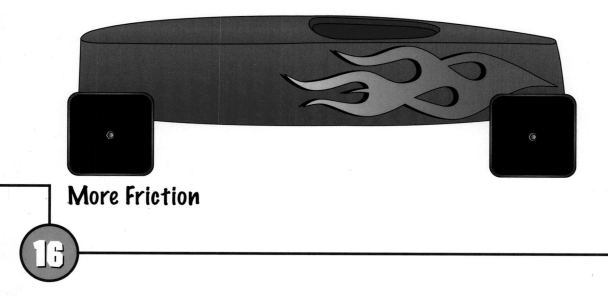

More Friction

Less Friction

WHEELED MACHINES

There are many kinds of wheeled machines. Some, like bicycles and motorcycles, have two wheels and two axles. Other machines, such as skateboards and cars, have four wheels and two axles.

Can you name a machine that has more than four wheels? Can you name one that has only one wheel and one axle?

Humans burn calories when they exercise, or work. If the dad jogged beside his son for 30 minutes, he'd burn approximately 250 calories. His son riding the bike would burn only 70 calories. Thank-you wheels!

WHEEL SIZE

Wheels are round so they can roll and reduce friction. But, not all wheels are the same size. Machines come in different sizes, so wheels have to come in different sizes, too.

Can you imagine putting big truck wheels and tires on your roller skates? Likewise, it wouldn't make sense to put skateboard-sized wheels on a dump truck!

Small wheels have to rotate more times to cover the same distance as large wheels.

USEFUL MACHINES

Machines like the wheel and axle make our lives easier. Sometimes they show up in the most unexpected places. For example, did you know the screwdriver is a wheel and axle? The handle acts as the wheel when it is turned. The shaft is the axle.

Think about how doorknobs, pizza cutters, and faucet handles work. Take a walk around your home and see how many useful wheels you can find.

shaft

handle

GLOSSARY

axle (AK-suhl): the shaft or rod in the center of a wheel

complex machines (KAHM-pleks muh-SHEENZ): machines with many moving parts

friction (FRIK-shun): a force that slows two objects when they rub together

mechanical advantage (mi-KAN-eh-kul ad-VAN-tij): what you gain when a simple machine allows you to use less effort

wheel (WEEL): a round object that turns on an axle or rod

INDEX

WEBSITES TO VISIT

www.kidskonnect.com/content/view/99/27
www.edheads.org/activities/simple-machines
www.brainpop.com/technology/simplemachines
www.mos.org/sln/Leonardo/InventorsToolbox.html
www.mos.org/sln/Leonardo/LeosMysteriousMachinery.html
www.harcourtschool.com/activity/machines/simple_machines.htm

ABOUT THE AUTHORS

David and Patricia Armentrout specialize in nonfiction children's books. They enjoy exploring different topics, and have written on a variety of subjects, including communities, sports, animals, and people. David and Patricia love to spend their free time outdoors with their two boys and dog Max.